Spanish Words on the Road

By Julia Salazar

Gareth Stevens
Publishing

Please visit our website, www.garethstevens.com. For a free color catalog of all our high-quality books, call toll free 1-800-542-2595 or fax 1-877-542-2596.

Library of Congress Cataloging-in-Publication Data

Salazar, Julia.
Spanish words on the road / by Julia Salazar.
 p. cm. — (Learn my language! Spanish)
Includes index.
ISBN 978-1-4824-0368-8 (pbk.)
ISBN 978-1-4824-0369-5 (6-pack)
ISBN 978-1-4824-0365-7 (library binding)
1. Vehicles — Juvenile literature. 2. Transportation — Juvenile literature. 3. Motor vehicle driving — Juvenile literature. 4. Spanish language — Vocabulary — Juvenile literature. I. Title.
TH4811.5 S25 2014
468—dc23

First Edition

Published in 2014 by
Gareth Stevens Publishing
111 East 14th Street, Suite 349
New York, NY 10003

Copyright © 2014 Gareth Stevens Publishing

Designer: Sarah Liddell
Editor: Therese Shea

Photo credits: Cover, p. 1 (road) Andrew Zarivny/Shutterstock.com; cover, p. 1 (road sign) rnl/Shutterstock.com; p. 5 kurhan/Shutterstock.com; p. 7 trekandshoot/Shutterstock.com; p. 9 Pavel Lysenko/Shutterstock.com; p. 11 © iStockphoto.com/SWKrullImaging; p. 13 © iStockphoto.com/laughingmango; p. 15 George Burba/Shutterstock.com; p. 17 (deer) Vishnevskiy Vasily/Shutterstock.com; p. 17 (forest) Anatoliy Lukich/Shutterstock.com; p. 19 Noel Hendrickson/Digital Vision/Getty Images; p. 21 Alastair Wallace/Shutterstock.com.

Printed in the United States of America

CPSIA compliance information: Batch #CW14GS: For further information contact Gareth Stevens, New York, New York at 1-800-542-2595.

Contents

Español on the Road. 4

Follow the Signs! 6

Motorcycle on the Move 8

Through the City. 10

By the Water 12

In the Mountains 14

Through the Forest. 16

Read the Map! 18

Chao 20

Glossary. 22

For More Information. 23

Index 24

Boldface words appear in the glossary.

Español on the Road

We're going on a road trip. Let's practice Spanish words in the car! *Español* is the word for Spanish. The Spanish word for car is *carro*. Look in the box on each page to learn how to say the Spanish words.

Spanish = español (ehs-pah-NYOHL)

car = carro (KAH-rroh)

carro

Follow the Signs!

We'll follow road signs, or *señales*, to find out where to go. There are lots of cars on the road. I see an *autobús*, too. That's Spanish for bus!

---

signs = señales (sehn-YAH-lehs)

bus = autobús (ow-toh-BOOS)

señales

Motorcycle on the Move

There's a man on a motorcycle, or *motocicleta*. He wears a **helmet**, or *casco*. I wear a helmet to stay safe on my bicycle!

motorcycle = motocicleta
(moh-toh-see-KLEH-tah)

helmet = casco (KAS-koh)

casco

motocicleta

9

Through the City

We drive through a city, or *ciudad*. It's very big and very busy! We stop at a *semáforo*. That's Spanish for **traffic light**. There are many *semáforos* in a city!

city = ciudad (see-yoo-DAHD)

traffic light = semáforo (seh-MAH-foh-roh)

semáforo

ciudad

By the Water

We drive by a beautiful lake, or *lago*. There's a big *lancha*! That's Spanish for boat. I wonder where it's going?

lake = lago (LAH-goh)

boat = lancha (LAHN-chah)

lancha

lago

13

In the Mountains

Next, we drive through the mountains. The Spanish word for mountain is *montaña*. We go up, up, up a mountain! It's much taller than a hill, or *colina*.

mountain = montaña (mohn-TA-nyah)

hill = colina (koh-LEE-nah)

montaña

Through the Forest

We drive through a *bosque*. That's Spanish for forest. There are lots of tall trees. Look! There's a deer! The Spanish word for deer is *venado*.

forest = bosque (BOHS-keh)

deer = venado (veh-NAH-doh)

bosque

venado

Read the Map!

We're lost! We look at a *mapa*. That's Spanish for map. We drove down the wrong street, or *calle*! Let's turn around.

map = mapa (MAH-pah)

street = calle (KAH-yeh)

mapa

Chao

Finally, I see the *océano*. That's Spanish for ocean. Our trip is done. It's time to swim and play on the beach. *¡Chao!* That means "bye!"

ocean = océano (oh-SAY-ah-noh)

bye = chao (CHOW)

océano

21

Glossary

helmet: a hat made of a hard material to keep the head from being harmed

traffic light: a signal using red, green, and yellow lights to control the movement of cars, trucks, and other vehicles along roads

For More Information

Books

Blackstone, Stella. *Bear Takes a Trip = Oso Se Va De Viaje.* Cambridge, MA: Barefoot Books, Inc., 2013.

Lawless, Laura K., and Beth L. Blair. *The Everything Kids First Spanish Puzzle and Activity Book: Making Practicing Español Fun and Fácil.* Avon, MA: Adams Media, 2006.

Wightwick, Jane. *Your First 100 Words in Spanish: Spanish for the Total Beginners Through Puzzles and Games.* Chicago, IL: McGraw-Hill, 2007.

Websites

Common Spanish Phrases
www.insidetraveling.com/spanish.htm
Learn some words that will be handy if you need to speak Spanish on the road!

Travel Spanish
www.123teachme.com/learn_spanish/travel_spanish
Choose a subject and practice your Spanish vocabulary.

Index

boat/lancha 12, 13
bus/autobús 6
bye/chao 20
car/carro 4, 5
city/ciudad 10, 11
deer/venado 16, 17
forest/bosque 16, 17
helmet/casco 8, 9
hill/colina 14
lake/lago 12, 13
map/mapa 18, 19
motorcycle/
    motocicleta 8, 9
mountain/montaña
    14, 15

ocean/océano 20, 21
road signs/señales 6,
    7
Spanish/español 4
street/calle 18
traffic light/semáforo
    10, 11